Selected Poems

KATE CLANCHY was born and grew up in
Scotland, but now lives in Oxford where she
was the first City Poet. Her three award-winning
poetry collections, *Slattern, Samarkand*, and
Newborn, are represented here. In addition,
Kate writes for radio and is the author of the
much acclaimed *Antigona and Me*, a memoir,
and *Meeting the English*, a Costa Prize short-listed
novel. She won the 2009 BBC Short Story Prize,
and *The Not Dead and the Saved*, a collection
of short stories, is forthcoming from Picador.
Kate is a Fellow of Oxford Brookes University,
and Writer in Residence for the charity First Story.

Kate Clanchy

Selected Poems

PICADOR

First published 2014 by Picador
an imprint of Pan Macmillan, a division of Macmillan Publishers Limited
Pan Macmillan, 20 New Wharf Road, London N1 9RR
Basingstoke and Oxford
Associated companies throughout the world
www.panmacmillan.com

ISBN 978-1-4472-6344-9

A CIP catalogue record for this book is available from the British Library.

Printed and bound by CPI Group (UK) Ltd, Croydon, CR0 4YY

Visit **www.picador.com** to read more about all our books
and to buy them. You will also find features, author interviews and
news of any author events, and you can sign up for e-newsletters
so that you're always first to hear about our new releases.

for Matthew

ACKNOWLEDGEMENTS

Some of these poems first appeared in:
Anvil New Poets 2, ed. Carol Ann Duffy;
The Observer/Arvon Anthology, 1993; *Acid Plaid:
New Scottish Writing*, ed. Harry Ritchie; *Ambit*;
Critical Quarterly; *Magma*; the *Independent*;
the *Independent on Sunday*; *Poetry Review*;
The Rialto; the *Scotsman*; the *New Statesman*;
the *Sunday Times*; *Thumbscrew*; the *Times
Educational Supplement*; *Verse*; and *Writing Women*;
and were broadcast on Radio 3, Radio 4 and
the BBC World Service.

I am grateful to Simon Armitage, Colette Bryce,
Don Paterson and Matthew Reynolds
for their perspicuous edits.

Contents

Slattern

I leave myself about, slatternly,
bits of me, and times I liked:
I let them go on lying where they fall,
crumple, if they will. I know fine
how to make them walk
and breathe again. Sometimes at night,
or on the train, I dream I'm dancing,
or lying in someone's arms who says
he loves my eyes in French, and again
and again I am walking up your road,
that first time, bidden and wanted,
the blossom on the trees, light,
light and buoyant. *Pull yourself
together*, they say, quite rightly,
but she is stubborn, that girl,
that hopeful one, still walking.

Men

I like the simple sort, the soft white-collared ones
smelling of wash that someone else has done,
of apples, hard new wood. I like the thin-skinned,
outdoor, crinkled kind, the athletes, big-limbed,
who stoop to hear, the moneyed men, the unironic
leisured sort who balk at jokes and have to blink,
the men with houses, kids in cars, who own
the earth and love it, know themselves at home
here, and so don't know they're born, or why
born is hard, but snatch life smack from the sky,
a cricket ball caught clean that fills the hand.

I put them all at sea. They peer at my dark land
as if through sun on dazzling waves, and laugh.

The Wedding Guest's Story

Shortly after ditching me, a matter of weeks,
in point of fact, she bought a remarkable
backless dress and got hitched to an ex-army chap
who climbs up rocks on Sundays: not the sort,

that chap, if I might explain, to stop for stragglers
or to soak up sun. He'd strike for the top
in skin tight kit, lycra shorts and pick, straining
straps around the crotch. In spite of which,

I took the half-meant invite straight, sat tight
throughout, let that dress flash a foot of flesh
to the hushed cathedral, and in my mind
I slowly climbed the low, secret steps of her spine,

swung for a while on my rope in the tuck
of her waist, scrambled sweating, swearing,
over the slopes of her shoulder blades,
to slump on the summit, weak, sobbing with loss.

The Aerialist

When I finally dined with the aerialist,
I found him just a college gymnast,
fresh pressed East Coast boy dismissed
from frosty Dartmouth February last,

distinguished just by his wish to kiss
the topmost stripe of the circus tent, sniff
sugar mixed with sawdust, trodden grass, and seek
the chalky hand of the Only Candelabra Girl.

Let me lift a glass and drink to the quirk
that lets him fly, slick in tights and lycra,
nightly through the Gods, and crick my neck
to watch him spin his new wife high above me,

her roped mouth, her spotlit nose, and
candles in her fingers, candles in her toes.

Designs

Since the tragic death of your young wife
in that sudden conflagration of bush grass
on the curve of the coast road, since I attended
the closed-coffin funeral in my netted hat,
sent the tender, blotted letter you smoothed
with your square fingers to better feel
its understanding, since our holiday in Scotland
where you learned to love again, I have
applied myself to the plan of our dream house.

Our lounge, wide as the deck of a ship, runs
the length of the sea-view terrace, done out
in terracotta with a border of Greek keys.
The chairs are laid-back, Lloyd Wright, accessories –
largely chrome. Outside, at present, are ponds
and prairie grass. I am calling to ask your opinion
on the position of the porch swing, and if
that grass with its grand sweep of dry clean blades
could, in some small way, distress you.

A Married Man

The married man dreamt last night
of a house that someone'd left him:
the sort of house you have in dreams,

a thousand rooms, one corridor. He wandered
round alone, he told me, smiled
his quiet, inward smile. *And found*

a secret garden, high walled, locked, odd
velvet green. There, a window looked
towards the ocean. He flexed pale hands,

I had, he said, *the key.* His wife touched
their girl asleep, a lush and heavy animal,
and watched him, knowing, satisfied.

Nine Months

He grew thin as she grew great,
ran, got back in shape –
like when we met, she said
at first, but glimpsed,
stretching in the street light,
the silhouette of a boy
some years before that.

Further each night
he ran, and faster – despite
the growing winter dark,
the rounded weight
of black which pressed
on the sparse-lit, urban park –
would sprint at last

as if for the finish tape.
As if he could hone
himself to bone, fine
down to a blade, to a sliver,
like a knife to cut the cord,
she thought, or to slice
the air, and hover, flicker,

disappear –

Heroine

She dreams of disasters, daily, at her desk:
the clean tear of an earthquake; a vast,
relieving flood; sees her profile saved
on the lifeboat, bruises rouged across her cheek;

blinks as a thousand cameras
frame her gallant, grateful wave, feels
the furry flock of microphones
feeding on her words. Or sometimes

thinks of simpler deaths: friends,
charred outlines in the fast lane,
parents, wiped in tragic fashion,
leaving her the house, the fortune;

and while she often plans the funerals –
tissued tears, the veil, the hat –
she thinks more of the phone calls
in the bright frail aftermath, urgent voices

sorry now, saying *anything*, dying to name her need.

The Personals

The one with herpes sounded best –
who didn't mention Solvency,
nor *s.o.h.*, nor Arts Degree,
didn't say he'd *l.t.m.*
a younger lady, petite, slim,
n.s., South-East, for Arts Pursuits –
but talked of this secret sore of his,
his soiling, suppurative lust.

Men from the Boys

Imagine this man as a lonely boy:
at the biscuit-smelling, sour milk stage,
shirt misbuttoned, strangled tie,
pockets stocked with fists and secrets.

The inky boy in the front row desk,
who writes his name, address, adds
England, Earth, the Universe, concocts
a six month scheme for their general good;

gets dressed in robes to bury voles,
makes the cat a home that goes unused
or tries to help the birds with nests;
gives over spring to crushing flies

to keep a fledgling half alive; and spends
dank winter afternoons spinning
treacle over spoons or making tapes
of private jokes with laughter

added later. This boy writes runes
in milk on library books, and *Out,*
Forbidden on his door. You know
that if you grab him now

you'll hold a bag of kicking bones.
He wants no comfort, mother, home.
He'll work the whole thing out alone.

The Invisible Man

It was the bandages that book got right.
We're none of us quite here, alone –
the way we pat our cheeks at night
to check our flesh still clothes the bone.

Recognition

Either my sight is getting worse,
or everyone looks like somebody else.
A trick of the light, perhaps, or shadows

in this dark bar with its fancy candles,
but I think the girl in hippy sandals
could turn, and in a spin of bangles,

be a girl I know but somehow younger,
her before I even knew her.
Or the skinny boy in the Aran jumper,

hair in the nape of his neck like a feather,
could puff out smoke, be my first lover
pulling me, laughing, into the shower:

as if no one I knew had ever got older,
haircuts, glasses, or just wandered further
than I could follow, chose to bother;

as if through sheer short-sightedness,
I could recover, rewrite losses,
sift through face on face-like faces,

make one focus, crystallise,
pull towards me, recognise,
see themselves, once more, in my blue eyes.

Speculation

The papers promised an eclipse:
the moon's black disc distinctly,
slowly, pushed part-way across the sun,
as a counter for the highest stakes
is slid circumspectly on another.

They added I should only watch
backwards, through a cardboard box,
even supplied a diagram, numbered
those already blind. It rained
all afternoon, of course. It was not

till four o'clock that I went out
and saw, in the empty, silvered street,
a shadow on the shadowed light,
a scarf of dark, like smoke
from barricades of tyres. I thought

of how it is with us – I stare,
you turn away and flush, as if
from heat or a blinding glare.
We generate that sort of weight.
A thickening of the atmosphere.

The Acolyte

Though you swear you are not
Simeon Stylites –
wouldn't spend, as he did,
half your life on a pillar,
crane-still amid acres
of Antiochian desert,
surveying a perfect
circumference of sunset,
and nearer to God
by a clear sixty feet –

I have found myself lately
dreaming of pulleys,
of yard arms, of bundles
of rope, the number
of Tupperware beakers of cordial,
of wax-papered triangles
of potted-meat sandwich
that a suspended lunch bucket
could practically take.

And I sleep, in your absence,
turning and turning,
like the hand of a watch,
or a woman prostrate
at the foot of a glaring
white pillar, pursuing,
through noon and siesta,
the rotating shadow
of a foreshortened, athletic,
odd form at the peak.

Still

High pressure has ironed
the Atlantic, kept the same
air hanging until it thickens
to tissue paper laid
on watercolours. The oaks
are yellowed, foxed
like ancient books. Dead

leaves fill the paths
like wadding. The cliff bathes
a battered foot where
a small baffled boat circles
in flat water. Berries group
to fists on the sky, black
as scribbles in the margin.

I've been walking miles
over fields whose furrows
run to the cliff's edge,
down worn roads set
in hedgerows neat as beards.
Still, love hangs in my head,
and gathers, like a storm.

Dare

Yesterday, I breasted
the Atlantic while the day
stood by with held
breath shivering on
the cusp of autumn

the cliffs stretched
west as far as they dared.
I swam across the white
loosening noose of waves
a little further.

Poem for a Man with No Sense of Smell

This is simply to inform you:

that the thickest line in the kink of my hand
smells like the feel of an old school desk,
the deep carved names worn sleek with sweat;

that beneath the spray of my expensive scent
my armpits sound a bass note strong
as the boom of a palm on a kettle drum;

that the wet flush of my fear is sharp
as the taste of an iron pipe, midwinter,
on a child's hot tongue; and that sometimes,

in a breeze, the delicate hairs on the nape
of my neck, just where you might bend
your head, might hesitate and brush your lips,

hold a scent frail and precise as a fleet
of tiny origami ships, just setting out to sea.

Raspberries

The way we can't remember heat, forget
the sweat and how we wore a weightless shirt
on chafing skin, the way we lose the taste
of raspberries, each winter; but

know at once, come sharp July, the vein
burning in the curtain, and from that light —
the block of sun on hot crushed sheets —
the blazing world we'll walk in,

was how it was, your touch. Not the rest,
not how we left, the drunkenness, just
your half-stifled, clumsy, frightened reach,
my uncurled hand, our fingers, meshed,

— like the first dazzled flinch from heat
or between the teeth, pips, a metal taste.

Sex, Like Planes

Despite the taxied miles,
the turns, the circling dust
disturbed in vast propellers,
the growing drone
that whines, that aches,
the weight of metal plates,

there's this: this shift,
this point called flight.
We hang absurd in air
and see the earth is barely there —
far-off, a swatch of dark soft stuff
stuck with pins of light.

Overnight

Then I heard your breathing thicken,
whisper past my ear like the first
inquisitive gust of a storm on the roof,

and saw darkness press through the curtains,
mass there like burdened clouds, and felt
your fingers open in sleep on my shoulders,

settle close as the first snow lining the ground,
and a dream flicker across your eyelids,
swift as the twitch of dry leaves in the wind,

and slowly your sleep deepened, gathered,
filled the room, calm as the great feathery flakes
that spin and land, weightless, one on the other,

and your arm loosened around me, suddenly,
as a branch will yield and shed its shelf of snow,
and your head dropped, filled the curve of my neck,

just as such a drift might shift, and all night
your fingers brushed my skin, steadily changing
everything, like the levelled white we saw

in the morning, the lawn expectant as an empty page.

One Night When We Paused Half-Way

I saw you naked, gazing past me,
your face drawn tight and narrow
as if straining in harsh sun,

as if standing at some crossroads
surveying faceless fields of wheat.
One hand on the humming motor

counting the strung-out poles from home.

Double Take

I imagined that you'd miss me, thought
you'd pace your hardwood floor in odd
worn socks, watch the clock sit stuck,

get late to work, type my name *caps lock*,
press and hold *shift/break*, miss buses, meals,
or sit with fork half-way, lost, for minutes,

hours, sleep badly, late, dream chases, shake,
send fingers out to pad the pillow, find
my hollow, start awake, roll over, hug a gap,

an ache, take a walk, damp dawn, of course,
wrapped in a mac with the collar up, glimpse
a slice of face, tap a stranger's back, draw a blank;

as I have. Each time, I run to press your face
to mine, mine, shining with imagined rain.

Deadman's Shoes

Last night your ghost walked in at two,
tall, calm as a father with his evening drink,
turned his back and sat to peel one sock off,
then the other. I hardly stirred, just matched
your usual sigh to my own intake of breath,
and slept on, near you, comforted;

but woke late and looked for your shoes
dropped in first position on the carpet.
The deadman's brogues we bought
that day in Brighton, inners stamped
with the outline of an instep. I wanted,
very much, to put my hands inside them.

Patagonia

I said *perhaps Patagonia,* and pictured
a peninsula, wide enough
for a couple of ladderback chairs
to wobble on at high tide. I thought

of us in breathless cold, facing
an horizon round as a coin, looped
in a cat's cradle strung by gulls
from sea to sun. I planned to wait

till the waves had bored themselves
to sleep, till the last clinging barnacles,
growing worried in the hush, had
paddled off in tiny coracles, till

those restless birds, your actor's hands,
had dropped slack into your lap,
until you'd turned, at last, to me.
When I spoke of Patagonia, I meant

skies all empty aching blue. I meant
years. I meant all of them with you.

Guenever

For who would have Sir Galahad
who could have his battered troubled Dad?
Would swap that wholesome holy boy
who works out in the sun all day,
polishes his sword, his spurs, his pecs,
pores over texts and hands out tracts,
smiles kindly when I try to flirt –
for his saturnine slouch-hat Papa,
asleep with his head on his rusting armour,
scarred hand cradling a scar?

There are no flies on Galahad
though plenty buzz around his Dad.
Gal slow-mos through his martial arts:
his father fells three midges dead
with a single slap at his string vest.
And I have seen Sir Lancelot
snatch a moth from its lamp-bound orbit,
cage it in his palm adroitly,
blow it dusty, puzzled, free –
and, still, keep his eyes on me.

Young Galahad we leave to God –
but I tell you, sir, no woman, none,
who has known this father and his son
would not choose to sit by Lancelot,
ogle at him in his cups,
hear him blurt out blurry secrets,
sluice his desperation deeper;
believe that she alone could touch
the thing he holds beneath his shirt
– his cracked-wide-open hardnut heart.

Amore, Amore

(for Clare)

A man from the Altai Republic
is ideal, really. As he speaks
mostly the Altai tongue,
a sparsely-latined form of Hun,
and your Russian's distinctly slim,
you must talk in such Italian
as he can croon from opera.

And as his land is landlocked,
accessible, some summers only,
by steamer up the Yangtze,
by creaking cog-wheel railway
over hills as round as topiary,
by immemorial goat-track
with your trunk on your head,

you must roll up your hammock,
start that trek to the cliff top where,
between cloudbursts, you can gaze
at his mountain, watch his rare
Altai cheeses swing and drip
in their muslin, hear him whistle
the notes of *amore*, over and over,

and *amore*, *amore*, go echoing back.

To Travel

(after Gösta Ågren)

If you should go to Samarkand
you might find Scheherazade
reproduced a thousand times,
tinsel-clad, in gift shops,
and Al-al-Din's gold-plated domes
slung with Soviet tourist signs
and tarnished, on a brassy sky.

But staying is a kind of leaving.
From here, the fields of Oxfordshire
stretch already sovereign-golden.
And when the hay is rolled in bales
like wheels, and your eye runs on
black tractor rills to autumn's bare horizon,
there shall burn there Samarkand,

and Samarkand, and Samarkand.

All This Still

It seems that grass still grows, leg-deep,
through cracks in concrete, iron mesh, that in June
there's hay, flaxen, dry, on waste ground
and on building sites, shaded in with withered red;

that Queen Anne's Lace still nods its heads
by breeze block walls or barbed wire fence;
that bindweed reaches twisted fists
to tiny holds on rusty tins in rubbish heaps;

and on hot days, that children come as ever,
wade the grass, hear the vast and rustling hush
that sucks their shouts; and stretching up
to snatch their ball, hovering in the smoky sky,

still catch the scent of summer sweat:
wind-blown, heated, meadow-sweet.

The Bridge Over the Border

Here, I should surely think of home –
my country and the neat steep town
where I grew up: its banks of cloud,
the winds and changing, stagey light,
its bouts of surly, freezing rain, or failing that,

the time the train stuck here half an hour.
It was hot, for once. The engine seemed
to grunt and breathe with us,
and in the hush, the busker at the back
plucked out *Scotland the Brave*. There was

a filmic, golden light and the man opposite
was struck, he said, with love.
He saw a country in my eyes.
But he was from Los Angeles,
and I was thinking of another bridge.

It was October. I was running to meet a man
with whom things were not quite settled,
were not, in fact, to ever settle, and I stopped
halfway to gaze at birds – swallows
in their distant thousands, drawn

to Africa, or heat, or home, not knowing
which, but certain how. Shifting on the paper sky,
they were crosses on stock-market graphs,
they were sand in a hoop shaken sideways,
and I stared, as if panning for gold.

Foreign

Consider abroad, how closely it brushes,
stiffens your skin like the scaly paw
of a fake fur throw when you wake at four
in a cheap hotel; creeps in sly as the hand
up your thigh on the spiralling, narrowing
minaret steps, clammy and moist as the stump
of a limb that's round as a baseball bat
but soft as the skin on the pad of cats' paws.

Think of the smells, the insecticide soaked
through your rucksack, passport; the rubbery
mould on the inside of tents; the medieval streets
with their stink like a phone box; the rain
on the dust, that stench of damp dog; the rush
of iron fresh from the butcher's; the stale
of the coppery water in temples, the yellow
ringed puddles behind great beaten doors.

And noises, the multiple clicks in your mind
like a camera; the howling of prayers
tannoyed from towers; the orders,
the bargains, the beggar's *baksheesh*; flip
flop flip of doors on buses; shrieks
from quarrels you can't understand,
buzzes and flies, the sound of the crowd
rising like water left running for hours.

Above all remember how little this touches,
how by evening it's telly, just small people
miming their hunger and rage. Remember,
against the prospect of mountains, the slice
of a city glimpsed through a window,
to measure that peering in mirrors for sun tans,
those glances in darkened windows of coaches,
searching your face for the difference.

Burglar Alarm, E1

It seems to be something
they're used to ignoring
in the stalls, curry houses,
Pound-Busters for Housewives,
the glassy, funereal arcades
of the Whitechapel Waste,
East Aldgate, Brick Lane –
this pulsing alarm, saying
*opened and taken, broken
and stolen*, again and again.

And that, furthermore,
they give no time to pondering –
the grandsons of pogroms,
calling out prices, the Somali
women with shopping
and veils, the Bengali men
clasping hands in a bargain,
all stilled in the milk
of a mild autumn evening –
this modern conundrum:

whether the starlings
dispersing like gunshot
on the smoke-stack clouds,
the bloody sky,
have recently learned
to sound like a siren, or
whether the siren
is intended to mimic
the hierarchic, repeating,
screams of migration.

Mitigation

We think you know the secret places,
the ones you called, perhaps, *Big Sands,*
The Den, or *Grassy Hill.* They loom up large
behind your eyes. Those hands that stroke
your signet ring, were once, like ours, blunt-
fingered, small, and clutched at grass or clenched
a stone and loved the tender, ticking throat

of panicked bird or retching child.
You watched the films, played Dracula.
That doll was yours whose head came off.
You stored her up behind the fort, the patch
of dirt around her mouth. There's something
buried in the park, a shallow grave, a rotting
thrush. You know the place. And know

the swooping railway tracks and why
we stole a child, like sweeties, from the shops.
You twitch and feel the small wet thrill.
You balked, you bottled, ran, that's all.
We heard you from the Policeman's van.
We heard your hands, the short, sharp slaps
of grown-ups clamouring to get back.

Soap

Today on the box we'll watch
a baby sleep by bombs and know
she's safe: our hero's on her corner.

Here, buttered light falls always
on the garden and envy's a prop,
a bit part on the way to love
that's marked by tongueless kisses.
I love your strength she tells the man
in fancy dress. We understand.

The children play with sadness,
loss, as if with dolls; casually
swap parents. All doors lie open.
Crims are simple, dirty folk
who shoot with blanks,
and wounds are clean. They heal.

Here the dead come back
with different faces, are greeted
unsurprised. This is the place
we dream together, our fingers
on the buttons, fiddling with time;
this place where nothing hurts.

The Natural History Museum

They are glassed and boxed like childhood,
the dead creatures in their pastoral
dance: the grinning fox and pouting squirrel,
the ferrets in their stiff quadrille. Parents nod
and watch their children watch the bloodshed
always about to happen: the wee mouse
cower, the wildcat locked in a pointless
leap. It was Bosch, I think, who painted
the Cat padding into Eden with a small beast
limp in her mouth. A child smiles. Her father
aims a camera. He shoots, and does not ask
what the half-silvered hare asserts,
stopped on the cusp of change, forever
almost escaping, kicking his heels at the dark.

Cambridge

I think it's time it withered, let us go:
the teashops, pubs, the upright girls on bikes;
the bright young men in shadowed doorways
calling clever names in code;

this softened, cheesy, gracious place
that quaintly leans to love the lounging river,
breathe its vegetable scent;
that wraps itself in tender light . . .

It's time to say enough: it's stale,
it's done to death. Let Safeways come,
McDonald's, let concrete pour,
here where the thousand bluebells lie

and dream only of bluebells, being blue.

Timetable

We all remember school, of course:
the lino warming, shoe bag smell, expanse
of polished floor. It's where we learned
to wait: hot cheeked in class, dreaming,
bored, for cheesy milk, for noisy now.
We learned to count, to rule off days,
and pattern time in coloured squares:
purple English, dark green Maths.

We hear the bells, sometimes,
for years, the squeal and crack
of chalk on black. We walk, don't run,
in awkward pairs, hoping for the open door,
a foreign teacher, fire drill. And love
is long aertex summers, tennis sweat,
and somewhere, someone singing flat.
The art room, empty, full of light.

War Poetry

The class has dropped its books. The janitor's
disturbed some wasps, broomed the nest
straight off the roof. It lies outside, exotic
as a fallen planet, a burst city of the poor;
its newsprint halls, its ashen, tiny rooms
all open to the air. The insects' buzz
is low-key as a smart machine. They group,
regroup, in stacks and coils, advance
and cross like pulsing points on radar screens.

And though the boys have shaven heads
and football strips, and would, they swear,
enlist at once, given half a chance, yes,
march down Owen's darkening lanes
to join the lads and stuff the Boche –
they don't rush out to pike the nest,
or lap the yard with grapeshot faces.
They watch the wasps through glass,
silently, abashed, the way we all watch war.

Pathetic Fallacy

You can't get drenched, however much you wish it.
You could stand all autumn on our corner
stubborn as a lamppost, and watch drains fill
and then spill over, puddles stretch to dimpled floods,
and still not feel the rain run through you,
cooling, cleaning out. Your skin's too tight to let it.

You could wait till all your clothes had shrunk
to sodden sails and both shoes had split and curled
like flowers, your hair slicked down to water-weeds,
till your eyebrows dripped clear stalactites
to tide pools in your eyes, but your heart
would go on pumping the same muddy blood around.

For rain is not relieving, nor new either.
It's our own old wet reused, gone acid,
coming down still muttering its boring song of loss.
It pisses down, it spits, it clings like sweat gone cold,
and when its fingers mock our necks, old hurts,
like blackened rotting leaves, resurface in the drains.

Teams

I would have skipped the stupid games,
long afternoons spent chilled in goal,
or sleepy, scratching, in deep field,
leapt the sagging fence
and learnt, as others do, apparently,
from dying mice, cow parsley,

if it weren't for this persistent sense
of something – like the words to songs,
sung out on the bus
to matches, like my name on lists
on notice boards, shortened,
called across the pitch,

trusted by the ones who knew,
the ones with casual shoulders, cool –
that thing, I mean, that knack, that ease,
still sailing, like those hockey balls,
like sodden summer tennis balls,
right past me.

Adolescents

We bother them: we're here, and scarred, alive.
We didn't exit as we should have
on our first lost love, leave
a young head lolling in long-stemmed roses,
or five wet streaks on a hotel wall.

We get to them: we keep on breathing,
raise our battered heads to the tat
of another autumn morning.
Can walk, do, and cloud and cloud
their crisp new air with our cow-like sighing.

Can't Argue with It

These boys I teach wear gold like armour.
They hold up hardened hands of rings to flick
the shivering light like knives as they sit and rock

and kick. They wear their names, short cold sounds,
on gold chains at their straining necks; cross, lock
bare arms on thin young chests and rock and kick,

and draw thin breaths through narrow mouths.
I watch their feet, as they rock and kick, and hear
them breathe and ask them why, and what, and why.

The Pair of Them

First day back,
and they wait to tell me
of their long boys' summer: how they clocked
three thousand miles in their new old car,
spent Saturdays schlepping round
kitsch Southend, drove

uninsured and smiling
to the beach at Le Touquet. By August,
their parents were Post-It notes on a trembling fridge
at noon, and the bed, unmade since June,
lay rucked in candlewick,
sunlit dunes.

And then, these boots.
These high-sided butch-toed things,
with untied thongs and lolling tongues: two pairs,
the spit, but bought, they tell me, separately,
because there's nothing going on here,
just telepathy.

Long Boots,

with hooks,
are in this year.
Some look to take an hour
or more to criss cross precisely
from the foot, to loop,
tighten, tug the yard
of hard-gripped
cord. And

to untie,
peel slowly from
each thigh, each calf,
wrench off leather where it grips
tighter round the heel, the instep, over
the twitching nose of toes,
takes, I'd say, a mirror,
certain music,
days.

I like
their icy, skateboot
strangeness. That girl
for instance – watch her inch
to the edge of her perch, unconscious,
lost, to herself, to us,
in her marvellous
alien legs.

Rain, Book, Classroom

A storm shades the page
like a stage light, dimmed,
rain hammers hard on roof-felted tin,

and the children's cheeks
are bright as Christmas.
Down the soot-soft tunnels
of their fixed dark eyes,

down tracks as fine
as printed lines, black
on the blank winter fields
of the page, steam trains

to where we've never been:
a frontier town with one saloon,
a clapboard school
with stove smoke rising,

where a storm shades the page
like a stage light, dimmed,
where rain hammers hard on roof-felted tin.

Hometime

When my grandfather died he saw,
he said, not Death's bare head, but aunts,
his antique aunts in crackling black,
come to call him back from play.

My Grandfather

His head was grand and mottled as a planet.
There were no maps: his rage sprang up
mysterious as geysers. The continents
were dark where his several brothers
lived (though Uncle James from Africa
once showed up in the flesh) and if
there were, in the frozen poles, the hole
he'd put his father in, long ago, I never knew
nor dared to ask. He was munificent
and vast. This is all I know for sure:

Grandad looked like old Duke Wayne
and shot birds with the Earl of Cairn.
He had cigars and a Jaguar, and his father
was a gas fitter. He beat us all at dominoes,
but drew black/black one day and died.
Because of him we're not self-made.
He left us that, Aunt Katie's rug
and a drawer full of cashmere socks,
luxurious and muffling, easily worn to holes.

For Absent People:

(Andreas 1965–92)

We learn to live with people we have lost:
our ex-lovers, former wives, those friends
who married wrong. They send by post
the breath of distant lives, the odds and ends
of stories we once started. We do not mourn;
don't think they've gone, they live on in files
we keep to quote to new loves, sit on the lawn
in photographs with squinting, creased-up smiles.

But you went for real and we were bereft,
not just of you, but of the words, the ways
to mark your going. You had completely left.
Just this: I dreamt of heat on your last night,
woke drenched and calm and feeling light.

Deep Blue

(*in memoriam* John Blau, 1964–1991,
and for his widow, Jackie Molloy)

I was not surprised to hear how the rest survived,
were anthropologists in Vegas, parents
or beat poets, had turned heterosexual
and got tenure at Yale; how even the tortoise
we fished out of the turtle-tank
in that upstate, backstreet pet shop,
still trundles round, armoured and mechanical,
drearily alive, while you, you had died.

You were always the one everyone chose.
The athlete, the actor, the centre of the photo
with your arms on many shoulders. I can hear
your rapid, Disney laugh, see you
reading Shakespeare in a college letter jacket.
It was Indian summer, you strutted
on a wall, your intent, coiled back,
dark, mobile face, inhabiting the Fool.

It was the mechanism got me – the intricate
encroachment of the thing. A single night
in Texas! Nobody could die from that
unless somebody planned it, unless
Death crouched a long time at his chessboard,
working it out. Unless he called to you

in passing, patted the café seat beside him,
quaint, European, an old man in the sun.

Then offered easy odds and gambits
of top roles and turtles, hooked your knight,
sipped coffee, let his bishop slide,
chuckled and checked you, shut
his rheumy, hooded eyes. You were easily bored.
You must have laughed that laugh
and leant across, twitched the king, slapped
the clock and turned to the street, to the girls

and the flowers, stretched your basketball limbs
tucked your thumbs in your pockets,
young, young, all Bogart, American.
You would have smiled when he murmured
your name. And I am shocked when I imagine
the click of wood on wood, and your face
when you recognized the absolute design
of his swift and final black rook move.

When my Grandmother said she should never have left

New Zealand, land of her birth,
breakfast lamb-chops,
and frequent, casual earthquakes –
it frightened us.
To cast her net so very wide
over years, decades, lives –
was like a ground tremor starting,
spreading quick as misgivings,
wrinkling oceans, rumpling borders,
spiralling out of the southern hemisphere
to compass Moscow and the War,
lap at England, Hampshire, here.

And then to let the sonar rings
reach our feet and pass us,
loop us, to pull them back
with that single gesture,
uptailing me, my cousins, brother,
into new volcanic fissures,
dowsing my father, uncle, aunt
in the China Sea till they paled to thoughts;
letting all our books and paintings
bob to other hands, like jetsam,
to push even my grandfather under
with his Captain's hat, his careful letters;

to furl all this in her fist at the epicentre,
where she stood, fifteen,
a skinny, straight-browed girl,
waiting for plates to settle flat
on the dresser, her cup
to click in the dent in the saucer,
the framed map of the Empire
to sway back horizontal,
for everything to be
as if nothing had happened,
and then to toss the twisted paper
in the grate to light a fire, later –

that shook me.

Present

For you, each night, the detail of each day:
so take the light that fell on London
this evening when I was on
the suburban, steady-breathing train.
Tender but particular, it rendered
brickwork and new leaves distinct,
gilded allotments and long gardens,
backlit tar-paper sheds,
filled failures of verandas
with their intended, hopeful shape.

Caught the scarlet-chested builder
spading gravel in the mixer,
made him heroic, a war poster;
lent to blazered boys on platforms
blowing smoke rings bright as halos,
the child who trailed her sister
like a slow-to-take-off kite, to the one
hand-fasted couple, their flowered acne
and pram, to all their separate ritual
squabbles, an authentic air of idyll.

Later, take the contents
of each lit window that I passed,
that seemed, tonight, bright slides
of an ideal life, take the cool
of my arms without my coat,
on this, the first of no-coat days,
the warmth of the pub, and the glass
after glass of pure foam, pure gas,
the barman drew from the tap,
his laugh. And lastly take, my love,

the water main that burst and made
a fountain, this drab street Italian.
Adults, luckless since they are not us
stopped and tutted at the waste,
but the blast arched on regardless,
the top droplets golden in the lamp,
a flood of unstoppable coins. Take them.
I turned like Whittington, stood
with laughing children, still as Cortés
on his peak. I filled my pockets up.

For a Wedding

(Camilla and Kieran 9/8/94)

Cousin, I think the shape of a marriage
is like the shelves my parents have carried
through Scotland to London, three houses;

is not distinguished, fine, French-polished,
but plywood and tatty, made
in the first place for children to batter,

still carrying markings in green felt tip,
but always, where there are books
and a landing, managing to fit;

that marriage has lumps like
their button-backed sofa, constantly,
shortly, about to be stuffed;

and that love grows fat
as their squinting cat, swelling
round as a loaf from her basket.

I wish you years that shape, that form,
and a pond in a Sunday, urban garden;
where you'll see your joined reflection tremble,

stand and watch the waterboatmen
skate with ease across the surface tension.

Content

Like walking in fog, in fog and mud,
do you remember, love? We kept,
for once, to the tourist path, boxed in mist,
conscious of just our feet and breath,
and at the peak, sat hand in hand, and let
the cliffs we'd climbed and cliffs to come
reveal themselves and be veiled again
quietly, with the prevailing wind.

The NewHome Cabaret

'Tis not, as once appeared the world,
A heap confused together hurled,
All negligently overthrown,
Gulfs, deserts, precipices, stone;
Your lesser world contains the same
But in more decent order tame;
You, Heaven's centre, Nature's lap
And Paradise's only map.

– From 'Upon Appleton House' by Andrew Marvell

Upon No. 30

This house has seen no architect.
You aren't supposed to squint
at its magnificence, blink
at its postmodern wit, but,
as you walk home with lowered head,
glimpse it, brick and whole and low,
from the corner of the noisy road,
and nod, be comforted.

It was boshed up to fit
such space as could be bought for it
and stands with elbows doucely tucked
inches from the neighbours' path.
It was shaped, if shaped at all,
on the idea that a house should have
one front parlour and one back,
two window eyes, its own front door.

No wall is straight or angle right,
for it was measured out by feet
placed heel to toe in tightrope style,
while estimates of heights were made
with bricks and string and one shut eye;
someone lay flat to calculate
a bed-length in the upstairs room,
reached out to add a wardrobe's width –

someone rather short, in fact.
We've grown since then –
this home for ten Victorians
will barely fit the two of us.
Let's go in, and hope a house
built from dirt with man's bare fists
has learned by now a woman's habit
of giving out, and being elastic,

so that the bowed wall will curve
a little more to let us breathe,
and the sloping floor will send
me on my office chair swivelling back
to meet your arms, and love rise
through each plaster pore, irreparable
as damp, and spread its spores
on every joist, invisibly, perpetually.

The NewHome Cabaret

Though we mean to plane
the walls to bone, pare the floorboards
bare and stain them dark, expose
expanses of Old Oxford bricks, raise
the grain in the tongue and groove,
to polish, bleach, limewash the lot
in the best spare modern style

we shall leave the 'fifties cooker
grinning where it stands.
It's labelled *NewHome Cabaret*,
the enamel sink is *Leisure*:
we like their cool design, bold notes of chrome
and the suggestion of undressing
in their aluminium names.

Underlay

Because we like to get things plain
we've hacked all day at nails and prised up
tacks and peeled and rolled and stacked
the soft strata of the floor. Now we sit on them,
a squashed pyramid of futures, and rest
our feet on the pale ghost-rug

the final oilcloth left. It was light to lift,
worn to the weft, but, where we scraped off
the dirt, still pink, still printed with chinoiserie:
a little lacquered bridge so clouded grey
with working boots that it no longer reached
the jasmine-cloaked pagoda.

It's dark, and in the window frame we see
ourselves, floating on a plane of light, haloed
in electricity, strange as if that first family
had looked up to see, briefly before them,
milk-skinned and alien, unimaginably large,
the future, fortunate, children of no war.

Hardboard

Grace Ethel Coombes covered up
the banisters and fireplaces,
the panels of the doors
in August, nineteen fifty-four
according to the crumpled *Mirror*

wedged in the bedroom chimney
behind the high-gloss paint
and hardboard, the tiny copper nails.
She was the aged daughter of this house.
Modern Housewives' War on Dust

the paper said, and *A Retraction*.
I tugged it out to see the picture,
and an avalanche of ash
fell in my lap and on the top
flopped the skeleton of a bird. Its skull

snapped off and lay wide-eyed.
A starling, or perhaps a thrush,
but shrunk to archaeopteryx.
Its wings were long white fingers,
stretched out to me in prayer.

Grace Ethel must have heard it fall
and thrash: a rush like love, at first,
then a nagging, migrainous pulse,
then a flutter like a faulty valve
in the chimney's hidden ventricle;

and pitied it, of course, but how
could she let that black
and headlong ball of soot fly out
to take its chance of air and light
or a swift bright death against the panes?

Dust

We've stripped this house to dust,
my love, the walls have pores like nibbled cake,
the ceilings crumb like icing;
the wood-wormed boards are light
as *langues de chat*, sugared with plaster.
And if you gather up the stuff,
and sift it from hand to hand,

you can see that of the larger grit,
bits must be brick and scraps of slate
from the gables and the chimney stack,
and since the wind blows east,
parts are shaved from St Mary's Church,
with one millionth, perhaps,
from the Holy Land or the Blue Mosque;

while of the finer, whiter stuff,
that silts our teeth and lines the bath,
some must be, already, us,
with a larger portion rubbed
from Miss Grace Coombes and all her folk
who lived here long enough to shed
themselves a hundred times at least.

Now we've sealed one room
with a skin of paint, knocked the worst
between the boards, laid a mattress
on the sloping floor. The heating ticks.
The ceiling shifts. Something leaks
behind the light, falls on our sheet, sparse
as the first sand in an upturned hourglass.

Customer Care

The man from Pickford's Movers
has wrapped my ancient tin-opener
(bought from Price-Busters
and greased with years of tuna)
in six layers of tissue paper
and a corrugated tube.

On this same principle
were Tutankhamun's viscera,
liver, kidneys, and brains,
bottled in four amphorae
and placed in alabaster
serpent-and-jackal-headed sculptures

of narrow, swaddled gods
which were huddled together
and left to gaze for all eternity
at each point of the compass
from the plump circumference
of a hieroglyphed pink pot.

Neither Pickford's nor Egyptians
consider it their place
to discriminate in packing
or in any way pass judgement
on what is vital to the new life
and what is obsolete.

The Mirror

The day we bought and gilded it,
it lay like a lake in my tiny flat,
showed us, as we rubbed its surface,
a stock of lover's secrets –
grasping hands, dark nostril gaps,
our pendulous strange undersides,
all front-lit, like a Lucien Freud.

Here, we've left it propped, let it
catch us out in bits – eyes bruised
with soot, hair aged with paint,
balletic legs on wobbling steps –
until now, the day to set it straight.
We're up against the glass, nose
to nose with our doubled selves.

I'm acting as the brace, spread-eagled
over the fireplace. You're on a chair,
mouth full of screws. We shake
with so much luck and glass, the risk
of arching past ourselves in showers
of shards and ancient mercury.
I shut my eyes, and feel the weight

go from me. You pull back my arm
and show me us. Fixed-up, framed,
hands raised and clasped – the Arnolfinis
at a football match. Behind us,
new-painted walls recede,
finished, levelled, green. The cat
curls his tail at the vanishing point.

The Tree

The apples are already ripe
on the tree Miss Coombes left us.
The tree is bowed almost to the ground.
I hadn't understood till now
the cold weight of them, or how
they crowd each branch in pairs,
yellow, round as Chinese lamps
on a ceremonial highway.

Dusk, and you're coming home.
I imagine your bike's dynamo
drawn like a fuse through
the darkening streets, to light
our house as now, all down our road,
the lights go on – the gold
of bulbs in potting sheds, ingots
of a hall, back bedroom, stair.

We live here now, and though,
elsewhere, a girl is leaning
on a carriage window, her finger
twisted round the rucksack packed
with everything she owns –
this is enough. We are
the lights, the lights, the lights
the trains flick by in the dark.

Newborn

A Sequence

One, Two

The camera has caught me
in a church doorway, stooping
to fasten what must be

my old cork-soled sandals,
their thick suede straps,
that dry, worn grip at heel

and instep. I'm smiling
downwards, pinkly
self-conscious, and above me

the arch is an extraordinary
blue. New – the whole place
was just lime-washed, azure

and sapphire rough-brushed
over moss. It stood in the moist heat
at a confluence of rivers –

I've even noted their names,
and the date, which says you, love,
are perhaps ten cells old.

In the humid space beneath
my dress, my body is bent
in the small effort of buckling,

the sag of my stomach briefly
leant on my thigh,
and, at the crux, in the press

of my nerveless places, you
are putting me on, easily,
the way a foot puts on a shoe.

Scan

They showed me on the screen
some star lit hills, a lucky sky,
then, resting among haar-filled fields,

a settlement round the outlet
of a phosphorescent river, all low windows
flickering with early electricity.

And they pointed out with a line of light
a hub like the start of a knotting city,
like a storm in a weather front, coalescing.

Under Weigh

In the last month I would cycle
each dusk round the meadow,
watching the rabbits hop briskly
away from the wheel. This was May
and the hay grew knee-high, thigh-high,
and I scythed through it – past
whippets and walkers, slender,
meandering lovers – thinking
of the physics of ships, how a keel
cuts best through deep waters
under a certain pressure of freight.

Pang

Forget the last weeks beached
in Joanna's garden watching
the snails gluily labour
up the inside arch of the trellis
and smash from the apex
eight feet to the ground, also
the dirt taste of raspberry-leaf tea.

You came for me early, like a keen
first date, announcing yourself
with an eager, even over-familiar,
uncle-ish hard tweak at my waist.

Driving to the Hospital

We were low on petrol
so I said let's freewheel
when we get to the hill.
It was dawn and the city
was nursing its quiet
and I liked the idea
of arriving with barely
a crunch on the gravel.
You smiled kindly and
eased the clutch gently
and backed us out of
the driveway and patted
my knee with exactly
the gesture you used
when we were courting,
remember, on the way
to your brother's: *I like
driving with my baby*,
that's what you said. And
at the time I wondered
why my heart leapt and leapt.

Driving Home

I want you to know
it was your father
picked you up when
you were crumpled
and warm as a handkerchief
drawn from his pocket,
and your father who walked
you out of the maze
of the hospital while I
flapped largely behind,
and your father who
tucked you into the car
and chose the exit
unerringly and drove
us home evenly, slowly
as though we were nosing
through floral, curious
crowds, as if the car
were an Ambassador
and we were rich
suddenly, tremulous, old.

Love

I hadn't met his kind before.
His misericord face – really,
like a joke on his father – blurred
as if from years of polish;
his hands like curled dry leaves;

the profligate heat he gave
out, gave out, his shallow,
careful breaths: I thought
his filaments would blow,
I thought he was an emperor,

dying on silk cushions.
I didn't know how to keep
him wrapped, I didn't know
how to give him suck, I had
no idea about him. At night

I tried to remember the feel
of his head on my neck, the skull
small as a cat's, the soft spot
hot as a smelted coin,
and the hair, the down, fine

as the innermost, vellum layer
of some rare snowcreature's
aureole of fur, if you could meet
such a beast, if you could
get so near. I started there.

Infant

In your frowning, fugitive days, small love,
your coracled, ecstatic nights,
possessed or at peace, hands clenched
on an unseen rope, or raised in blessing
like the Pope, as your white etched feet
tread sooty roofs of canal tunnels
or lie released, stretched north in sleep –

you seem to me an early saint, a Celt,
eyes fixed on a celestial light, patiently
setting the sextant straight
to follow your godsent map, now
braced against a baffling gale, now
becalmed, fingers barely sculling
through warm muddy tides.

Soon, you will make your way out
of this estuary country, leave
the low farms and fog banks, tack through
the brackish channels and long
reed-clogged rivulets, reach
the last turn, the salt air and river mouth,
the wide grey sea beyond it.

When You Cried

I sat and mourned, let you
thrash on my lap like a choking
fish. The way your soft spine
chain-linked, grew strong!

It was as if you were a salmon
and our arms were nets, as if
you were searching upstream,
upstream, for the dark pool

you came from, for your
proper ground. I thought
you'd seen through us, that
you knew this wasn't home.

Rejoice in the Lamb

At night, in your shift, fine hair upright,
you are my tiny Bedlamite,

admonishing the laughing crowd
with your pale, magisterial hands,

or roaring out like poor Kit Smart
how blessed, electric, all things are.

The Burden

I'd never have thought that this would be me,
content to tote the baby homewards
answering, rook-like, his hoarse calls,
counting the haws on the bare claw branches,
the rose hips shining like blood.

And you'd be the one at the gate left staring
at the cloud-shadows etched on the copper water,
the flooded fields we couldn't cross.
That I'd let a hundred yards stretch between us.
How bright this thin, bisected moon.

Aneurysm

When my father heard his friend
was dead, we sat a while and talked
of traffic: how cars clog
each by-way now, every road
you think you know. We were quiet,
and I lit the lamp. I thought

I could hear the cars outside,
bashing, lowing, rank on rank.
There'd been a crash, my father said,
and his friend had walked out,
shaken, saved. It was hours
before the blood-clot got him.

I held my baby on my lap. It was
dark, it was the winter solstice.
We said there is no such thing
as the right route or a clear passage
no matter where you start,
or how you plan it.

Plain Work

We should knit, Joanna,
or tat, however that is done.
These winter afternoons –
we should drop wood eggs
down socks, or hold
long knotted wefts between us.

We should have stuff
to show for this: for the days
we've sat together, waiting
for our babies to get over
a tooth, a want, a croupy fever;
to get an hour older.

Yards of it by now – enough
to fill this room, surround us.
Great rolls of random rainbow
cloth, twisted, lumpen, fine,
the bright wool stitched in,
stitched in, line by line.

Ararat

Winter of floods – winter of broken banks
and radio warnings and me
running down the road with the pushchair screaming
and a cloud helicoptering low behind me.

Remember even the genteel Cherwell
bursting, the Isis brimming, swelling under
its muddy meniscus like a body rolling
in sleep in a blanket? The times you came home

to find the armchairs floating, the carpet
a quicksand, the tables at unprecedented levels,
the baby awash in his Moses basket and me
bailing madly as he rose to the ceiling?

Yet here we all are, no worse than muddy, and look –
the hills emerging, exactly the same, casual as knees.

Find

When he's at his grandparents'
we can't sleep without him
rolled in his blankets,
two floors below us:

the heart of the house,
muscular, unconscious;
deep in our wrappings
our golden scarab.

Dark, Dark

He is calling down the night,
the way he calls out
next door's dog and sees
the word grow ears
and eyes, emerge on heavy
loping legs, a furry
manifest of name.

The dark will have
a lion's neck. He'll ride
its muscled back all night.

Learning to Walk

He's on the brink – all day
hanging on a table's edge,
nosing his feet – his fists – his grand
round *Sèvres* head, slowly
into nothing.

        All my life
I've smashed cups and wept,
and this is forever too, I guess;
this liquid heart, this sense
that he's the water, I'm the glass.

In a Prospect of Flowers

So he can walk. We follow
his little trolley out
across the greening garden,

and hope he'll always learn
like this: the random
swipe of feet firming

over months and weeks
to these determined
stiff short steps. Next,

we'd have him sing, or paint,
or play – trumpet, violin –
not scales, you understand, but

jazz, the stuff cut off from us,
so schooled, well-versed . . .
Look out! He's making off.

You go before to sweep the way,
I bend in his mower's wake.
His brahmin's pace. Our scholars' gait.

Moon, O Moon!

The heaps of leaves he loved
are gone. Now we have
the moon: a thumbprint
on noon airmail skies; in the night,
a bitten coin; hungover
in the morning, a party lantern
in the trees.

(My metaphors approximate
the sphere of his apostrophes.)

The View

So much of this is cowpoke work,
so much of this is gates and getting
through them – there could be a mountain
rearing above us, there could be a city
hung above the cloudline and still
I'd be keeping my eyes on your footprints,
still I'd be steering this flock home.

Do you think there is a mountain,
my darling, my poppet, stooped there
on your stick like the village elder?
Is it upside down in the depths
of that puddle? I shall flop down
beside you, straight-legged and muddy,
stir up a sunset in the altering oil.

Storm

So, here
at the height
of this summer
of wrong, in this wrong
hour of this most wrong day
in the heart of the week which went
awry, now while the rain washes
the window free of every
roof we know, of every
tree, you and I, small
one, have come
to an impasse.

You're red,
half-dressed, push-
ing your car up the hill
of the chair. I'm white, flat
out in a field of trousers, listening
to the wind – which is your own twin,
darling – howl for its place, for
its proper season, and bash
our doors and walls
with its enormous
kitchen roll tube
trumpet.

Rhymes for September

Your wrist sticks an inch from this spring's sweater
as you pick the first curled leaf from the water.
And the turn-ups on your trousers are two turns shorter,
and the sun's sunk to some kind of bathchair
angle, and a cat's-paw breeze is riffling my paper,

flipping the dateline over and over. Where are
they now, our gold afternoons at the lido? This year
I meant to wax them over, store the picture
of us in pellucid water, two akimbo flies in amber,
all winter in the soot of my mind's cellar.

But only last night, now I come to remember,
I heard the boy next door start his meander
up the first four notes of a new trumpet air.
It was *When the Saints* all spring and summer,
now it's *How Many Roads?* And there's my answer.

Our Balloon

I'm drawing
a hot-air balloon.
A canopy with felt-pen
stripes, a scratchy pencilled
basket. He says it must have
people in it, so I put him in, two
dots, a grin, and since he goes
nowhere solo, add his father
as a beard, myself as curls,
and on request and out
of scale the cat's two
ears and one
stroke
tail.

There.
He stares.
I think

about balloons:
the roar up there,
the chills, the helpless
mild boredom. Do you talk?
I think you can't. I think you
must shade your eyes and mime
towards some house, some farm
shrunk to a diagram, and shout
to the wind, '—onderful time.'
Us in balloon, he says. We are.
It is. And since he'll not
be parted from it,
I fold
up

his balloon
and tuck it
in his pocket.

The Dream of Warm Things

All the way back he talks about
the calf we saw in the field,
a Jersey calf with a thick cream coat,

which he was scared of, in fact,
when it stumped over
the hummocked grass to greet us,

knots in its furry, flyblown ears.
We watched it take its milk, and now
he wants to make sure

of its mother and father,
wants to call them down from
the rapidly distancing hills, wants

to wrap the calf in a blanket,
press it safely under cover, the way
Peter and Mopsy are pressed

in their book, neat in their linen,
rush-lit bed: the way his
whole world, lately,

is honeycombed with dreams
of warm things, mice
about their tiny humid lives, spiders

snug in spouts. I stroke the soft
hot dome of his forehead, the furrow
where the line will come,

and say *yes* to the calf
in his unlikely blankets, the private
familial life of the flea. I say

all of them are warm enough, all
of them are tucked up now, listening
to their mothers' stories

as the globe turns to the enfolding
darkness, as we draw up
and stop the car in the dark.

Miscarriage, Midwinter

For weeks we've been promising
snow. You have in mind
thick flakes and a thick white sky;
you are longing to roll up
a snowman, to give him a hat
and a pebbly smile. We have ice
and I've shown you, under
the lid of the rainwater barrel, a single
spine forming, crystals pricked
to the delicate shape of a fir, but
what can I say to these hard
desolate flakes, dusting our path
like an industrial disaster?
It's dark, but I'm trying to scrape
some together, to mould just
the head of the world's smallest
snowman, but it's too cold
and it powders like ash in my hand.

Dumping the Christmas Tree

takes both of us, it transpires,
reeling to the park with our irregular
burden, strewing dead spines
like smoke from a censer. Afterwards,
wordless, we bash each other clear
of the needles and tinsel,
Punch and Judy in the freezing air.

What do they know of marriage –
these passers-by staring, these
thin joggers crunching hollow
ice in the puddles? You and I,
we have lived in Helsinki,
we have walked over
the dark rime of the sea.

Mendings

He is sitting in the bath,
telling the story where his ball
becomes a balloon, and after

long fugues involving aeroplanes,
tractors, oh, all the grand
detritus of space, bangs

into the moon and we mend it,
mend it, we have to get
moon glue. I'm squatting on the floor;

trying to let his voice, the net
of ripples in his hands, the line
of shine on his golden hair, thread

past my rocking legs, my arms
locked in temper. The other night
I told a friend,

a woman I've always liked,
that *happy ever after* is just
another room, and you're still

you in it; and now I'm wondering
even if that's true – but
she was saying she'd lost

her man, and when she smiled
I saw her teeth were old,
had that yellow sheen like Bakelite

or piano keys, and I thought
of her last eggs, the womb
staying empty, folded

like an evening purse, and anyway
on nights like these my heart
creaks on its fault lines like damp

in the marble veins of a fracture.
He's still talking.
He's saying the sun is in pieces,

and the stars are in pieces,
and we are mending them,
mending them, all of us

and the cat are mending them,
gluing them and now we are tired
and we're going home for a rest.

I gather him up, his limbs
weighty and nacreous,
hold him close and damp in a towel.

From the window I show him
how, beyond the reflection –
where he is an angel leaning

out of a cloud – the winter
has widened the black of the sky.
There are the stars, and the moon,

unshattered, smudged tonight
like an ovum setting out
on its glamorous journey.

He puts his arms around my neck
when we walk down
the stairs, and they're steep

but that one time we slipped,
I sat down quick as déjà vu
and we were OK, OK. Now

my arms are full of him
and his head on my neck
is heavy and full. O moon glue,

sun glue, star glue. Surely,
across the universe,
the blocks of dark pulling always

randomly apart, I have seen
your glaucous threads
reaching, tenuously re-joining

The Other Woman

I am running to meet her,
now, the girl who lives on her own,
who has in her hand the key to her own
hallway, her own bare polished stair, who
is clacking down it now, in kitten heels, swearing,
who is marching over envelopes marked with a single name,
who is late, can be late, sleep late, forget things,
who tonight has forgotten hat, gloves and
umbrella, and is running not caring
through the luminous rain.
What shall we say?

Shall I slip off
my coat and order cold wine
and watch myself sip it through
the long row of optics, arching my back
on the velvet banquette? And pick up the wit,
the moue of the mouth as we pass jokes like olives?
And say the right thing and stand up for my round,
tapping the bar with a rolled-up twenty,
tipsy, self-conscious, a girl,
a vessel of secrets, so
carefully held in?

Or down just one glass
and see stars and the whole
room go smeary, have nothing to say
and say all the same – apropos of nothing,
in the middle of everything – *You don't understand.*
What happens in birth is someone slips from your side, someone
full-sized. Will she yawn, get her bag, start tucking
her fags in when I get out his photo,
say *Look, look how he's grown,*
all by himself, he has grown
to the size of my life?

Stance

Now I sit my child on the jut
of my hip, and take
his weight with the curve
of my waist, like a tree
split at the fork,
like lovers leaning out of a waltz.

Nothing is lost. I was never
one of those girls
stood slim as a sapling.
I was often alone at the dance.

Index of Titles

Index of First Lines